Snakes

Written by Adrienne Mason

Illustrated by Nancy Gray Ogle

KIDS CAN PRESS

WILDLIFE SERIES

Kids Can Press

For Angus — AM

For my son, Connor — NGO

I would like to thank Patrick Gregory, Professor of Biology,
University of Victoria, for his manuscript review and consultation.

Kids Can Press acknowledges the financial support of
the Government of Ontario, through the Ontario Media
Development Corporation's Ontario Book Initiative; the
Ontario Arts Council; the Canada Council for the Arts;
and the Government of Canada, through the BPIDP, for
our publishing activity.

Published in Canada by
Kids Can Press Ltd.
29 Birch Avenue
Toronto, ON M4V 1E2

Published in the U.S. by
Kids Can Press Ltd.
2250 Military Road
Tonawanda, NY 14150

www.kidscanpress.com

Edited by Stacey Roderick
Designed by Marie Bartholomew
Printed and bound in China

The hardcover edition of this book is smyth sewn
casebound.
The paperback edition of this book is limp sewn with a
drawn-on cover.

CM 05 0 9 8 7 6 5 4 3 2 1
CM PA 05 0 9 8 7 6 5 4 3 2 1

**National Library of Canada Cataloguing in
Publication Data**

Mason, Adrienne
   Snakes / written by Adrienne Mason ; illustrated by
Nancy Gray Ogle.

(Kids Can Press wildlife series)
Includes index.

ISBN 1-55337-627-7 (bound)
ISBN 1-55337-628-5 (pbk.)

1. Snakes — Juvenile literature. I. Ogle, Nancy Gray
II. Title. III. Series.

QL666.O6M36 2005   j597.96   C2004-903901-6

Kids Can Press is a Corus™ Entertainment company

Contents

Snakes

Snakes are long, slender animals without arms or legs. They move around on their bellies. Most snakes are terrestrial — they live on land — but some live in the water.

Snakes are carnivores. This means that they eat other animals for food. Some snakes are venomous. Venom is a poisonous liquid that snakes use to kill their prey and to defend themselves.

Snakes can be as thin as a pencil, like this blind snake, or thicker than a fire hose, like this anaconda. Some snakes stretch longer than the length of a playground slide.

Western blind snake

A snake's skin is dry, not slimy.

Yellow anaconda

Snakes are reptiles

Snakes are related to lizards, turtles, tortoises, crocodiles and alligators. All of these animals are reptiles.

Reptiles are vertebrates. This means they have a backbone. Reptiles breathe air with lungs. They also have a tough skin, which keeps them from drying out.

Reptiles don't have fur or feathers to keep them warm. Instead, reptiles change their body temperature by moving to where it is warmer or cooler. When reptiles are cold, usually in the morning, they lie in the sunlight. This warms them up so they can begin to hunt for food.

About one-third of all kinds of reptiles in the world are snakes.

Sometimes reptiles can get too hot. When this happens, they move into the shade or a cool spot such as a burrow in the ground.

Rosy boa

Where snakes live

Snakes live almost everywhere in the world except on some islands and where it is very cold, such as high mountains and the Antarctic. There are more than 2500 species of snakes in the world. About 500 different species live in North America.

Since snakes need warm surroundings to heat up their bodies, more snakes live in hot places. The world's largest snakes grow where it is warm year-round. These snakes don't have to take time to warm up each morning so they have more time for hunting than snakes that live in cold places. And since they spend more time eating, snakes in warm climates can grow to be very large.

Snakes that live in cooler places are usually smaller, like the garter snake. It is able to live in cool places and can live as far north as the Northwest Territories in Canada. The garter snake is the most common snake in North America.

Common garter snake

Where common garter snakes live

North America

Common garter snake

SNAKE FACT

There are no wild snakes in New Zealand, Newfoundland, Ireland or on many other islands.

Snake homes

Snakes live in forests, fields and deserts. Some even live in swamps or oceans. They live where they can find food and shelter. This is called their habitat. Some snakes hide under rocks and logs or live in holes in the ground. Others spend most of their time in trees or water.

Rough green snake

Snakes that live in trees often blend in so well that they look like a branch.

The shape and color of many snakes help to keep them hidden in their habitat. They stay very still waiting for prey to pass.

Western diamondback rattlesnake

Northern water snake

Some eastern screech owls will catch a blind snake to put in their nest so it will eat insect pests.

Many snakes spend their time in the water, where they feed on fish and other animals.

Tiny blind snakes live underground and feed on insects. Blind snakes are not really blind, but their eyesight is weak.

Texas blind snake

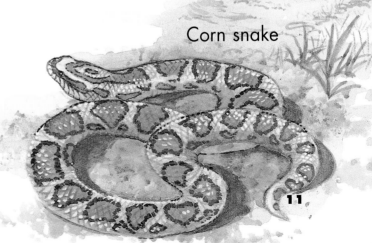

Corn snake

Some snakes live near people on farms, in parks and even in cities.

Snakes in winter

In the colder parts of North America, snakes change their behavior to survive the winter. In the late fall, snakes move into burrows, caves or deep cracks in rocks, where it is warmer. The snakes coil up and don't move. Their breathing and heart rate slows down, and they don't eat. This is called hibernation.

Even snakes that hibernate may not survive the winter, though. If the winter is unusually cold, many snakes will die.

As it warms up in the spring, those snakes that survived the winter become active again.

Sometimes hundreds, or even thousands, of garter snakes share a winter hibernation site.

SNAKE FACT

Snakes usually return to the same place to hibernate each winter.

Snake bodies

Snakes are built for moving and feeding without arms or legs. This is a common king snake.

Tongue

Snakes flick their long, forked tongues to smell the air and ground. This helps snakes recognize the scent of prey, enemies or other snakes.

Teeth

Slender, sharp teeth are curved back so that it is hard for prey to escape.

Eyes

Eyes help snakes see objects close to them. Snakes do not have eyelids. Instead, their eyes are protected by a clear scale called a spectacle.

Fangs

Venomous snakes, like this rattlesnake, have long, hollow teeth called fangs. Fangs pierce the prey's skin and inject venom.

Jaw

A snake's jaw opens wide enough to swallow prey larger than its own head.

Internal organs

The liver, stomach and lungs are long and narrow to fit into a snake's slender body. A snake's stomach stretches to hold large prey.

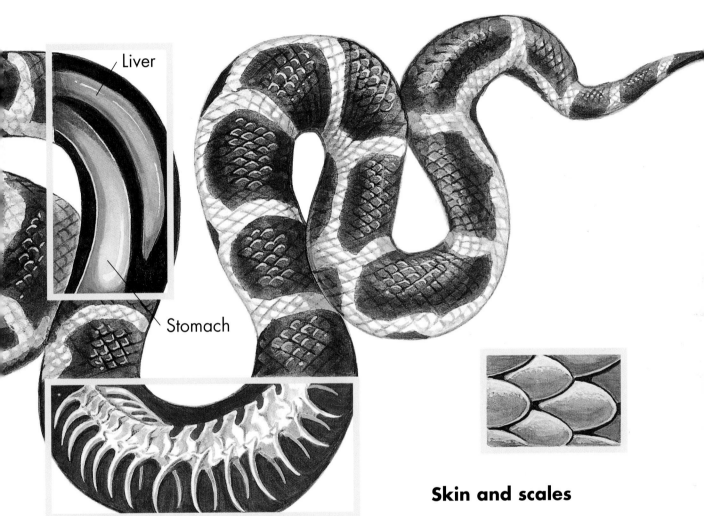

Liver

Stomach

Skin and scales

Snake skin is very flexible so it will stretch if a snake swallows large prey. The thick, waterproof scales, shown here, protect the snake's skin.

Spine and ribs

A snake's spine bends easily as it moves. Each bone in the spine is connected to a curved pair of ribs.

Snake senses

Snakes use their senses to find prey and avoid enemies.

Most snakes see well close-up. They react quickly to any movement they see.

Snakes can hear some very low sounds, but they also sense movement and vibrations through their skin. When animals move, they make the ground vibrate, or shake slightly. The vibrations can help snakes sense where a nearby animal is.

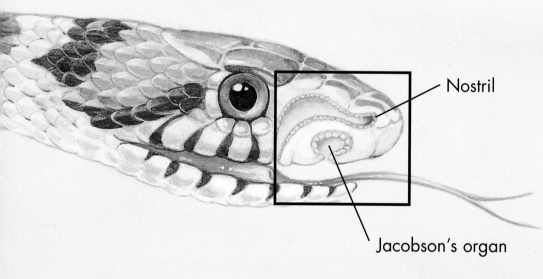

Nostril

Jacobson's organ

Two small pits in the roof of a snake's mouth are part of the Jacobson's organ. The snake flicks its forked tongue out to gather scents from its surroundings. Then the snake pulls its tongue back into its mouth. The scents go into the pits, and the Jacobson's organ helps the snake figure out whether food, enemies or another snake is nearby.

Heat pits

Some snakes, such as this rattlesnake, have special heat-sensitive pits between their eyes and nostrils. These pits recognize changes in air temperature. If the snake senses heat, it knows prey is nearby. The pits help snakes hunt even when it is dark.

Copperhead

Snake food

Snakes catch and eat animals such as mice, frogs, insects, slugs, rats, birds and even other snakes.

Snakes often wait motionless to surprise passing prey. They can wait for hours or even days. When prey does come by, snakes strike quickly.

Small animals are eaten alive. The snake grabs small prey in its sharp teeth and moves its jaws to force the prey down its throat.

Large prey needs to be killed first so that it doesn't struggle and injure the snake. Some snakes use venom to make their prey helpless. A few minutes after the snake bites, its prey dies. Venom also helps the snake digest its food. It can take several days for a snake to digest a large meal.

Eastern milk snake

Other snakes kill large animals by coiling their bodies around the prey. Then the prey suffocates, or stops breathing.

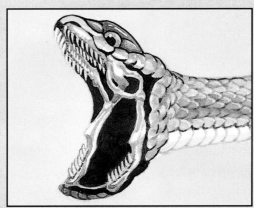

Snakes can't chew, so they must swallow food whole. The bones in a snake's jaw are loosely joined so that its mouth opens wide enough to swallow large prey. The two sides of the lower jaw are joined by an elastic strap that lets it stretch even wider.

How snakes move

Snakes have different ways of moving, depending on their habitat.

Most snakes travel by moving their bodies into S-shaped curves. The scales on the snake's belly grip the ground and help the snake push itself forward. Snakes that swim also use this S-shaped motion.

Eastern coral snakes

Sidewinder
rattlesnake

On soft ground such as sand, snakes travel by sidewinding. The snake coils its body up and pushes it forward and to the side.

When a snake climbs trees or digs into burrows, it pulls and pushes its body like an inchworm. First, it coils up its front end to grip the side of the tree or burrow and then pulls its tail forward. Then, it grips with its tail and pushes the rest of its body straight ahead.

Black rat snakes

Baby snakes

Some types of snakes lay eggs. Others give birth to live babies. Either way, baby snakes look just like tiny copies of adult snakes.

Female snakes find places that are warm, damp and hidden to lay their eggs. This keeps the eggs moist and safe from animals that eat eggs.

The shells of snake eggs are not hard and brittle like a bird's egg. Instead, they are tough and flexible. Depending on the species, as many as 50 eggs are laid at a time. Most female snakes leave the eggs as soon as they have been laid, but some species guard and warm their eggs.

After six to twelve weeks, the eggs hatch. A baby snake uses a tiny egg tooth to slit open the shell.

Western hog-nosed snakes

Many species of snakes that live in cool climates have live babies. The eggs are kept warmer in the mother's body than on the cool ground. Babies that grow inside their mother are also better protected from predators than eggs laid on the ground are.

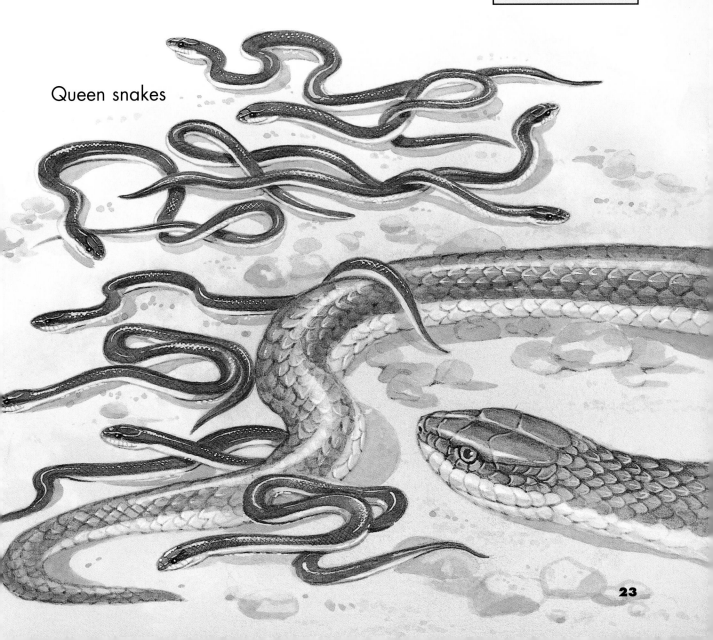

Queen snakes

23

How snakes grow and learn

In a few species, mother snakes hide with their babies for a few days after they are hatched or born. But most adult snakes do not take care of their babies. As soon as baby snakes are hatched or born, they are on their own.

Baby snakes know how to hunt as soon as they are born. At first, baby snakes eat small prey such as insects or worms. As they grow, they begin to hunt larger animals. Venomous snakes have venom at birth. Their venom can be even stronger than their parents' venom.

As snakes grow, they shed the outer layer of their skin. First, a snake grows a new layer of skin underneath its old one. The old skin then loosens. The snake rubs its head against rocks or bark so its skin starts to roll back. The snake then wriggles out, leaving its old skin turned inside out.

Young snakes shed about three times a year. Adult snakes shed their skin once or twice a year.

Eastern fox snakes

How snakes protect themselves

Snake predators include owls, hawks, crows, skunks, raccoons, turtles and other snakes. Snakes will bite predators if necessary, but they have other ways of protecting themselves as well.

Many snakes defend themselves by staying hidden. The coloring and patterns on their bodies blend in with rocks, dirt or tree branches.

When threatened, snakes often give warnings before biting. Some coil up their bodies and hiss loudly. Others release a bad-smelling scent. Rattlesnakes shake the rattles on the end of their tails. Other snakes try to look larger or more threatening by thrashing around or rearing up. They also might pretend to strike. Some venomous snakes are very brightly colored in bands of red, yellow, white and black. This warns predators to stay away.

Western diamondback rattlesnake

SNAKE FACT

Hog-nosed snakes sometimes roll over and play dead if disturbed.

Snakes of the world

Africa

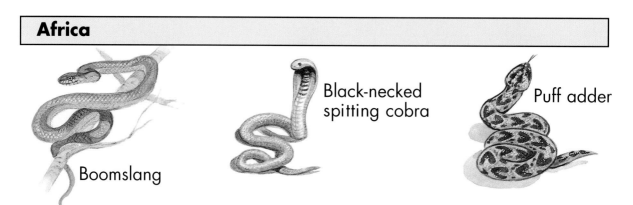

Boomslang

Black-necked
spitting cobra

Puff adder

Asia

Reticulated
python

King cobra

Monacled cobra

Australia

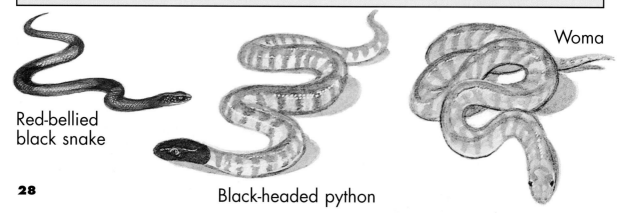

Woma

Red-bellied
black snake

Black-headed python

Europe

Grass snake

European adder

North America

Western hog-nosed snake

Striped racer

South America

Emerald tree boa

Boa constrictor

Green anaconda

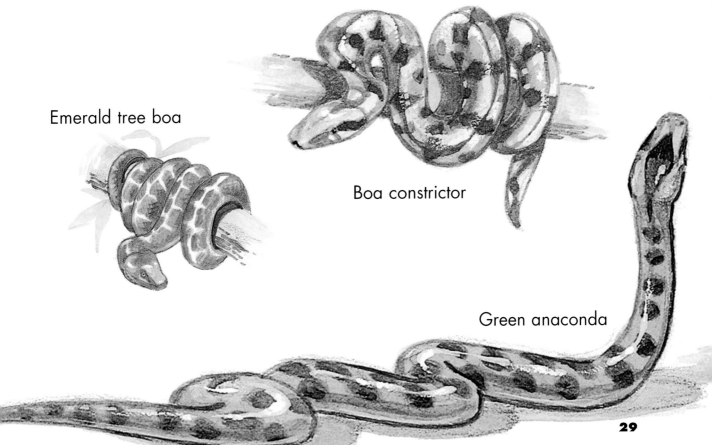

Snakes and people

Snakes help people. They eat insects and rodent pests, such as mice and rats.

Some snake venom is used to make medicines that help people who have had strokes or have other illnesses. Venom is also used to make antivenin, which helps people and animals such as cattle that have been bitten by snakes.

Some people are afraid of snakes, even those that aren't venomous. Because of this, snakes are often killed needlessly.

Often people are afraid of snakes because they don't understand them. Many people are working to change this. Scientists study snakes and their habitats. Other people show snakes to children and adults, and teach them about the lives of snakes. These people also help save the habitats of snakes so that snakes will have food and a safe place to live.

Words to know

antivenin: medicine used to treat snake bites

carnivore: an animal that eats other animals

habitat: where an animal lives

hibernation: a deep sleep during winter. Hibernation helps animals save energy and survive the winter in cold climates.

Jacobson's organ: a sense organ that helps snakes identify smells

organ: the soft inside parts of an animal, such as the heart, lungs and stomach

predator: an animal that kills and eats other animals

prey: an animal that is captured and eaten

spectacle: a clear scale over a snake's eye

terrestrial: lives on land

venom: a poisonous liquid used by some snakes to kill prey or predators

Index